I0035886

Endure the Tiger

Negotiating to gain ground

Endure the Tiger

Negotiating to gain ground

Leonie McKeon

DoctorZed
Publishing
www.doctorzed.com

Copyright © 2020 by Leonie McKeon

All rights reserved. No part of this book may be used or reproduced by any means, graphic, electronic, or mechanical, including photocopying, recording, taping or by any information storage retrieval system without the written permission of the publisher except in the case of brief quotations embodied in critical articles and reviews.

Books may be ordered through booksellers or by contacting:
www.leoniemckeon.com

1st edition published by DoctorZed Publishing
www.doctorzed.com

ISBN: 978-0-6485361-6-1 (hc)
ISBN: 978-0-6485361-7-8 (sc)
ISBN: 978-0-6481315-1-9 (ebk)

A CiP number for this title can be found at the National Library of Australia.

Cover image © Trish Pollock

Because of the dynamic nature of the Internet, any web addresses or links contained in this book may have changed since publication and may no longer be valid. The views expressed in this work are solely those of the author. The author does not dispense financial advice or prescribe the use of any technique as a form of guarantee for financial or business viability without the advice of a qualified financial advisor, either directly or indirectly. The intent of the author is only to offer information of a general nature to help you in your business. In the event you use any of the information in this book for yourself or your business, which is your constitutional right, the author and the publisher assume no responsibility for your actions.

Printed in Australia, UK and USA.
rev. date 30/11/2020

Contents

Acknowledgements

The act of writing a series of books is a process that requires the support of many people, without whose encouragement and practical assistance this venture would not have been possible. As always, I want to thank my publisher Dr. Scott Zarcinas at DoctorZed Publishing, editor Hari Teah, and designer Trish Pollock at BrandArk, whose skills have contributed so much to this book.

Special thanks to Suzanne McKenzie for her excellent research skills, which have made such a positive contribution to *Endure the Tiger: Negotiating to gain ground.* In addition to reading endless drafts, my sister Jennifer McKeon has remained continuously optimistic in relation to the entire *The Dao of Negotiation: The Path Between Eastern Strategies and Western Minds* series of books.

Last, and in no way least, my heartfelt thanks go to Shelley Rogers, who has used her skills in organisational psychology to help me think through the intricacies of each story and the most relevant examples to accompany them. Shelley has been consistent in her support for me and for the *The Dao of Negotiation* project, for which I am endlessly appreciative.

"Ponder and deliberate before you make a move."

Sun Tzu, *The Art of War*

Leonie's Journey Continues

*A*fter winning the Entrepreneurial Scholarship with the University of Adelaide in 1998, I launched a company assisting Western business people understand how to deal with Chinese business people. My objective was to implement my realisation that Mandarin Chinese is just different, not difficult. I did this by designing an easy-to-learn Mandarin language course for business people, the basis of which was my Mandarin Sounds Table. This Mandarin Sounds Table uses Pinyin, which is the phonetic system used to assist the pronunciation of Mandarin. My Sounds Table became the basis of my online course **www.pronouncemandarin.com**. I developed Chinese cultural awareness workshops, Mandarin language tuition, and translation and interpretation services, along with consultancy services for Western businesses wanting to understand how to do business with Chinese people.

I owned and operated this business for fifteen years, working across an array of sectors. I also employed several Chinese staff, with up to eight staff at any one time. Even though my staff had been university-educated in Western countries there were still significant cultural differences which were not taught as part of their university degrees. Learning how to employ Chinese staff and understanding these cultural differences in the workplace gave me the hands-on knowledge to help other Western businesses successfully employ Chinese staff.

Having Chinese staff work in your business provides a wealth of knowledge when your business is dealing with China. However, it can be difficult to use this knowledge if you do not know much about Chinese culture. Two years into running my business, I was introduced to the 36 Strategies which are derived from Sun Tzu's – *The Art of War*. I had heard about *The Art of War* and was aware that this was an important text on many Master of Business courses. Even though the 36 Strategies are 2,500 years old, they are still recognised as the core of understanding Chinese thinking and negotiation. This was something I had to know, to advise Western business people on how to deal successfully with China.

I began to locate contemporary business examples for each strategy, so that Western business people would be able to see how these strategies were being applied on them. The 36 Strategies are idioms, just like Western idioms such as 'don't cry over spilt milk.' People understand idioms as cultural pieces within their language, with several layers of meaning. I researched the 36 Strategies for a year, interviewing as many Chinese people as possible to articulate exactly what these strategies really mean. After gaining a deep understanding of the 36 Strategies, I designed workshops and gave keynote presentations at conferences. In 2013 I wanted to take my knowledge of the 36 Strategies to the next level. I sold the business I had operated for fifteen years and reinvented myself as a China-educated strategist so I could focus totally on the 36 Strategies. This series of books *The Dao of Negotiation* became a necessary component in helping people develop an understanding of how these strategies are applied in the contemporary business world. To understand how Chinese people think and negotiate in the business environment it is crucial to have some understanding of the 36 Strategies. As I have demonstrated in *The Dao of Negotiation* series, the 36 Strategies can be used in any Western business environment.

The Pinyin System

*F*irst developed in the mid 1950s, the Pinyin system is a phonetic system used to pronounce Mandarin Chinese. Literally translated as 'spell sound', Pinyin was created to transcribe the sounds of Chinese and to allow native English speakers to pronounce and read them without being required to memorise the characters. Although it was created for non-Chinese people to learn Mandarin pronunciation, it is important to know that many words are not pronounced the same way that they are pronounced in English. For example, 'c' in Pinyin is pronounced 'ts' as in 'bits' instead of 'c' as in 'cat' in English. Essentially, each Chinese sound is its own syllable, and each Chinese character is its own Pinyin syllable. Not only is Pinyin useful in learning the accurate pronunciation of Mandarin, it is also a great tool to use when inputting Chinese characters onto computers or smartphone devices.

In addition to the pronunciation, four tones are used in Mandarin to clarify the meaning of words. This means that two words with the same Pinyin spelling may have completely different meanings, depending on the tone that is used to pronounce the word.

Fortunately, Mandarin Chinese is highly contextual in that, provided the context in which the word is being used is clear, the meaning is highly likely to be understood by a Mandarin speaker irrespective of the accuracy of the tone. Readers are encouraged to go to **www.pronouncemandarin.com** to learn Mandarin Chinese pronunciation and many useful words and phrases.

Strategies for Gaining Ground

*I*n Book Five, *Endure the Tiger: Negotiating to Gain Ground* you will learn strategies that take advantage of the situation to move you forward in your strategic moves. These are the **Strategies for Gaining Ground**. This book will describe Strategies 25 - 30, which are used when you need to be strategic in your approach to gain ground.

The gaining ground strategies aim to gain an advantage in any opportunity through exploitation of the opponent's weaknesses. The purpose of the gaining ground strategies is to remove the control from your opponent. To be successful it is important to be clever in the approach, by using methods which include diversion, confusion, and entrapment. The use of strength and speed in the implementation of the gaining ground strategies is likely to allow you to control or even defeat your counterpart.

Strategies for
Gaining Ground

Replace the beams with rotten timbers
means "to destroy the structure on which the opponent depends and then rebuild and take control"

Disrupt the enemy's formations, interfere with their methods of operation, change the rules that they are following, and go contrary to their standard training. In this way you remove the supporting pillar, the common link that makes a group an effective fighting force.

---

*I*n ancient China, Emperor Fu Jian of Qin planned to attack General Xie Shi of Jin. The emperor's decision to attack was due to the growing strength of Jin. By eliminating the strong but smaller Jin, Qin would be safer. In anticipation of the commencement of battle, General Xie Shi's army positioned itself along the riverbank on the opposite side to Emperor Fu Jian's troops. Each side waited for the other side to make the first move. Everyone was hesitant, because they were all experienced enough soldiers to know that trying to fight in the water was difficult and would place them in a vulnerable position.

To break the impasse, General Xie Shi sent a messenger to Emperor Fu Jian. The message proposed that General Xie Shi's army cross the river, on the proviso that the emperor order his army not to attack until the river crossing had been completed. Emperor Fu Jian told the messenger to tell

General Xie Shi he agreed to this plan. However, he was not telling the truth. Emperor Fu Jian saw this as an opportunity to attack General Xie Shi's army when less than half the army had crossed the river. In order to make it look l he was adhering to the agreement; the emperor ordered his troops to step back from the river to give room for the general's army to begin the crossing.

General Xie Shi was a clever strategist and had anticipated Emperor Fu Jian's response to the plan. To apply Strategy Twenty-Five – **Replace the beams with rotten timbers,** General Xie Shi first '*disrupted the enemy's formations*' by proposing an idea that resulted in the emperor moving his troops away from their strong position by the river. He also '*interfered with their methods of operations*' by infiltrating Emperor Fu Jian's troops with men disguised as imperial troops, looking exactly like Emperor Fu Jian's army. These men spread a rumour that the movement away from the riverbank was in fact a retreat because Emperor Jian expected he would be defeated. As a result, the emperor's army broke their formation and was in chaos. By the time Emperor Fu Jian realised what was going on and ordered his generals to get the troops back into formation, it was too late. Amidst this chaos, General Xie Shi quickly crossed the river and attacked Emperor Fu Jian's army. Strategy Twenty-Five was successfully applied because General Xie Shi's troops defeated Emperor Fu Jian's army. By moving his army back from the river, the emperor had '*interfered with their methods of operations*', and the disguised men had successfully '*disrupted the army's formations*'.

When Strategy Twenty-Five is applied, the strategist takes advantage of any opportunity or vulnerability their opponent presents. The strategist may also provoke a situation within which they are then able to '*remove the supporting pillar*'.

Negotiating with Chinese People

EXAMPLE ONE
Strategy Twenty-Five in action (against you)

In this scenario, you go to China on a trade mission with twenty other businesses from your country. Your product is a large range of vitamins. From your research the health sector is a fast-growing market in China. You visit Shanghai, and during this visit decide to go independently to some networking events. You want to explore opportunities beyond those presented by the trade mission organisers and gain your own experiences of China.

Your objective is to locate a reliable distributor who is well connected and can distribute your products into reputable stores. In the first instance, your plan is to export your products into Shanghai, and then once you have learnt about the market in China and developed a solid relationship with your chosen distributor, you plan to venture into other locations in China.

The first networking function you attend by yourself is a breakfast where you meet two Chinese businessmen who are very keen to talk about the distribution of your products. You have a unique logo and stylish packaging which is attractive to the two businessmen. You arrange to meet the next day to discuss how you can work together. They pick you up in an expensive European car and take you to an exclusive restaurant for lunch. Then they take you to a high-end supermarket, telling you confidently they can get your product into outlets like this. They are well-connected and speak very good English. This makes the situation much easier for you because you speak no Mandarin Chinese.

You sign a deal for the distribution of ten of your best-selling products into Shanghai, planning to introduce forty more products once you have established the distribution process. After returning to your country you send the initial products to these distributors. There is not much communication from them, except to say they have received the products. They tell you everything is fine, although the interest in your products is rather slow. They explain to you that this slow uptake is normal because they are new products. You feel confident that your products will sell because they are unique within the Chinese market, the logo is appealing, and the quality is of a high standard. After one month of exporting your products you decide to travel to China. When you arrive, the two Chinese businessmen who are your distributors apply Strategy Twenty-Five on you.

They apply Strategy Twenty-Five by '*interfering with your methods of operation*'. They tell you that something important they need to attend to has come up, and they will resume operations in six weeks to two months. During this time, they put their own products onto the market, using a design that is very similar to yours. They changed your logo slightly, so it is not an exact copy, and the vitamins they buy come from a factory in China. These distributors have '*changed the rules that you are used to following*'.

The distributors have '*removed your supporting pillar*', which is your logo. You considered your logo to be the competitive advantage in the China market. You are now left without a distributor, and your product has been replicated in a way that looks similar to the original, even if the quality is not the same. These distributors have been very clever to stay within the boundaries of copyright laws. They have successfully applied Strategy Twenty-Five.

EXAMPLE ONE
Guarding yourself against Strategy Twenty-Five

In this scenario, to guard yourself against Strategy Twenty-Five, when seeking out further opportunities, attending at least three networking events would have been wise. This would also have widened your opportunities of meeting potential distributors and enabled you to conduct research on these distributors.

These two Chinese business people had limited experience in importing products into China. When visiting the supermarket, you could have requested to meet the manager, to see for yourself if they were well-connected with the store. You may also have returned to visit the store by yourself to confirm that the person they introduced you to was indeed the store manager.

Being picked up in an expensive car is a common method Chinese business people use to create a good impression. Consider they may have hired this car for the day merely to impress you, and to give themselves 'face'. 'Face' is explained in Book Three – *Lure the Tiger: Negotiating in confronting circumstances.* Chinese business people are generally astute, opportunistic entrepreneurs who look for cost-effective ways of doing things, so you must be aware that you are always playing the game of negotiation.

When the distributor informed you that something important, they needed to attend to had come up, it would have been a good idea to negotiate a time limit, such as two weeks.

Have as many agreements in place as you can in order to protect your product. Not immediately accepting what the Chinese business people request, and instead pushing back a little, also demonstrates that you are not subordinate, and less likely to be an easy candidate to have Strategy Twenty-Five applied on you.

Example Two
Strategy Twenty-Five in action (against you)

In this scenario you are exporting fish oil into China. You have produced a high-quality product in your own country and have spent many years establishing yourself in the domestic market, where you have a very good reputation. When you commenced exploring the China market for your product you saw that the potential would be very large. To ensure you would not be completely overwhelmed, you set up a solid supply chain into China with a reliable distributor. Your distributor has a significant presence in the health space in Guangdong and Yunnan Provinces. This distributor also has good connections into retail outlets and hospitals. You had heard that hospital connections are very difficult to get in China, so you feel fortunate to have found this distributor. You have signed a five-year contract for your distributor to have exclusivity to sell your product into the two provinces. For two years, the export of your product there were no concerns, and everything ran smoothly. You were careful not to give your distributor exclusive rights to sell your product across the whole of China, as a result of this decision you felt that you had not placed yourself in a risky position, because they only had the distribution rights for two provinces in China.

After two years of dealing with this distributor you learn that they have entered a business relationship with another fish oil producer from another country. On hearing this news, you immediately conducted some research into this other product. From your research you believe it is an inferior product to yours, and therefore you are not that concerned about such competition. You have always seen your competitive edge as being in the quality of your product.

On one of your trips to China you do some independent research to see where your fish oil product is being sold. You realise that the inferior fish oil product has a more prominent position on the retail shelves, which may explain the fall in your sales over the past six months.

You meet with your distributor to discuss your concerns and when approached, your distributor applies Strategy Six – **Make a noise in the East and attack in the West** by shifting the focus of your conversation. Strategy Six is explained in Book One – *Tame the Tiger: Negotiating from a Position of Power*. You are aware of this strategy, and successfully keep them on track when addressing the issue of the way in which this inferior product that has gained a significant position in China. However, they have successfully applied Strategy Twenty-Five on you.

The inferior fish oil product has already entered the

market and is selling well. By distributing this similar yet inferior fish oil product, your distributor has '*interfered with your methods of operation.*' They have also '*removed your supporting pillar*', which is the quality of your product, and your competitive edge.

By successfully applying Strategy Twenty-Five, your distributor built a relationship with a more inferior fish oil company and is now importing this product for a much cheaper price. The distributor has given you an option that is not profitable, leaving you in the position of having to find another distributor. Due to the five-year contract you signed, your distributor also has exclusive rights to sell your product in two large provinces in China for a further three years. You will now need to spend time and effort dismantling this contract.

Example Two
Guarding yourself against Strategy Twenty-Five

Even if you have a solid relationship, it is a perfectly normal business practice in China for your distributor to search out other foreign products in order to increase their profit and product range. In this scenario it would have been good business practice to have at least one other distributor. Giving one distributor five years of exclusive rights to large provinces puts you at risk, by limiting what you can do in China.

If your distributor is aware that they are your only distributor in China then you are in a vulnerable position, as they will have control over the sale of your product. If you want to sell your product at the high-end of the market in China, then work with several distributors who operate in that space. Even if the distributors you meet have good connections to outlets for your product, this does not mean that they are the only distributors with good connections. There are many well-connected distributors in China. In order to guard yourself against Strategy Twenty-Five, you need to research the most appropriate distributors that suit your particular product. Finally, do not assume that Chinese distributors will use the same rules as the distributors in your country.

Key Points when Strategy Twenty-Five is used against you
- Look for several distributors who work in the market that suits your product.
- Recognise your vulnerabilities, then act to defend them by selecting your distributors carefully, and ensuring your contracts are not going to restrict your sales.
- Never become complacent when doing business in China – always remember you are dealing with expert negotiators.

EXAMPLE THREE
Enacting Strategy Twenty-Five

Strategy Twenty-Five is generally used when dealing with business people who have more resources or power than you. In this scenario you plan to export premium honey into China. Initially you meet with many different distributors, and discover that they do not supply upmarket supermarkets, which means your product's positioning would not be aligned with its price point, significantly affecting your potential profit.

You finally meet distributors in Shanghai who focus on getting high-value foreign products into upmarket supermarkets. Unfortunately, they are not interested in distributing your honey because your product is new into the market and has very little history. Many other foreign products have been welcomed by this distributor in Shanghai, and you realise this is because their product range has a long-standing good reputation with upmarket supermarkets in Shanghai.

You are very confident that your premium honey will sell well in China, even though it has only been selling in your own country for one year. To interest your preferred distributor in Shanghai you apply Strategy Twenty-Five. '*You change the rules that they are used to following*' by first going to smaller cities in China. These cities have fewer premium foreign products available, so your honey quickly becomes popular among the local distributors.

Having little competition, your product quickly gains a good reputation. After two years of selling into the smaller cities you once again approach the upmarket distributor in Shanghai about the possibility of importing your honey. You give them a strong presentation showing that several other distributors in China are importing your now popular product.

You tell the distributor that many people across China are now aware of your premium honey, and therefore it should easily sell in the upmarket supermarkets and food stores that specialise in selling premium foreign foods in Shanghai.

This application of Strategy Twenty-Five presents a likely future growth and a belief in possible high sales of your product to the distributor in Shanghai, which in turn will interest them in importing your premium honey.

Negotiating in a Western Environment

EXAMPLE FOUR
Enacting Strategy Twenty-Five

You work in a rehabilitation consultancy firm and have a good relationship with a large corporate insurance company that supports injured workers getting back into employment. In recent months, your referrals from the corporate insurance company have decreased. You are concerned, as your business income has decreased by a quarter. To rectify this, you commence the application of Strategy Twenty-Five. Firstly, you organise a meeting and invite the contact person from the corporate insurance company to visit your office. You discuss the specific needs of their clients. You let them know that with this information you will conduct a short training session with your team to ensure they are meeting the standards the corporate insurance company expect. As you have taken the time to meet with the contact person from the corporate insurance company and implemented a training session to meet their specific needs, they have more trust in you and your staff.

A few weeks later your contact person from the corporate insurance company contacts you because they are going on annual leave for a month, and do not have an internal colleague to cover for them during their leave time. They approach you, as their trust in your company has grown following your meeting with them and the implementation of the training session.

They ask you to come in and assist with their workflow while they are on leave. By meeting with them and implementing training for your staff to address their specific needs you have '*interfered with their methods of operation and changed the rules that they are used to following*'. By assisting the corporate insurance company while your contact person is on leave, you get the opportunity to refer rehabilitation work directly to your business. You have not only created trust so they continue to use your services, you are now in the forefront of their minds for when they may need extra assistance, and working inside their company gives you access to their client base, which means you can refer these clients directly to your company. In this scenario Strategy Twenty-Five has been successfully applied and utilised in several ways to benefit your rehabilitation consultancy firm.

Key Points when using Strategy Twenty-Five
- Plan to maximise your strengths to put yourself in a strong position.
- Make use of the information your customer or client gives you, regarding their needs.
- Be prepared to make a small concession or sidestep to reposition yourself to move forward.

Point at the mulberry tree but curse the locust tree *means "to convey your intentions and opinions indirectly"*

To discipline, control, or warn others whose status or position excludes them from direct confrontation, using analogy and innuendo. Without directly naming names, those accused cannot retaliate without revealing their complicity.

Sun Tzu was a famous strategist in China. In fact, the 36 Strategies are attributed to Sun Tzu's – *The Art of War*. Emperor He Hu was very pleased with the progress of the development of Sun Tzu's war strategies. He wanted to see a demonstration of how Sun Tzu's strategies would work when training a new group of army troops. For this demonstration he presented Sun Tzu with a group of 180 women who were not familiar with army behaviour, and said he wanted to see how the strategist would train these women to march in an army formation. Sun Tzu was confident he could do this. He divided the women into two troops and appointed one of the emperor's concubines to lead each troop of women. Sun Tzu gave the two women explicit instructions on how to lead their troops in formation. Then the drums played loudly, which was a signal to commence marching. The concubines had not followed Sun Tzu's orders at all and laughed when the drums played. He repeated the drums playing to signal the leaders to lead the troops of women. They laughed again and did not commence the marching. The next time this happened Sun Tzu applied Strategy Twenty-Six – **Point at the mulberry tree but curse the locust tree**. He was determined to show the emperor he was an excellent strategist. To *'discipline, control, or warn others'*, he had the two concubines beheaded. This action was done *'without directly naming names'* - although all the women were fully aware this had happened. He then appointed two more women to lead the troops as they marched in formation. He again gave explicit instructions on how to lead the troops to these newly appointed women. These new leaders explained the orders to their troops in detail, resulting in all the women marching in perfect formation. From this situation Sun Tzu had demonstrated in front of Emperor He Hu that he was an extremely competent strategist. The emperor was very pleased and appointed Sun Tzu as his own army's commander-in-chief.

As indirect communication is mostly the way Chinese business people communicate, Strategy Twenty-Six is often used in communicating a point of view as a way of saving 'face'. It is also a method used to make an example of those who do not comply with cultural rules, so others in the group will be intimidated into submission.

Negotiating with Chinese People

EXAMPLE ONE
Strategy Twenty-Six in action (against you)

Lobster is a popular high-value product to export to China. China's middle-classes are becoming accustomed to eating lobster at high-class banquets. A foreign seafood company is exporting their lobster to China. This is a family business and they have been dealing with a Chinese distributor for one year. The lobster product has been selling well in China. The senior members of the foreign lobster company do not see the need to learn the cultural rules when dealing with China. They perceive that their product is in such high demand there is no need to learn any of the cultural rules when working with a Chinese company.

Representatives of the foreign company have visited China twice since they started exporting their lobster. There are three managers from the company who conduct these visits. Two are senior family members. The third, a junior manager, handles the administrative details of exporting and is not directly involved in the business discussions such as price and delivery dates. The Chinese distribution company is aware that anything they tell this junior manager will go back to the rest of the team.

The Chinese company have ten senior staff who conduct trade negotiations and host dinners for this seafood company. The foreign company is visiting China for the third time, and their cultural skills are the same as they were on their first visit. The Chinese distributors are not impressed with the behaviour of the company's representatives and are reconsidering purchase of their product.

The foreign lobster company is complacent and under the impression that they do not have any competitors. They have caused 'loss of face' through not understanding Chinese cultural rules. When they first visited, the foreign company representatives were given business cards, which they merely glanced at before putting them in their pockets. When given a Chinese business card it is important to carefully read the card and to be seen doing so. During their second visit, when they were hosted at a dinner by the Chinese distributor, the foreigners consumed their drinks whenever they liked, as they would in their home country. At formal Chinese dinners it is culturally appropriate to wait for the host to make a toast and then everyone drinks together. The foreigners also sat where they wished around the banqueting table, ignoring the hierarchy. The hierarchal nature of Chinese business culture means there are appropriate places for everyone to sit, and guests must wait for the host to tell them where to sit at the table, in accordance with their status.

To ensure these cultural blunders do not reoccur the distributors applied Strategy Twenty-Six '*to discipline, control, or warn others*.' A member of the Chinese team met with the junior manager from the lobster company, telling her that her colleagues must be more culturally appropriate because their behaviour last time caused 'loss of face'. Prior to the next hosted banquet, she told her two senior managers that they needed to act in a more culturally appropriate way. Not understanding the application of Strategy Twenty-Six, these comments caused embarrassment and annoyance. They did not like hearing criticism so indirectly. They believed the quality of their product was enough and that they did not need to change their behaviour. At the next banquet they acted in the same way they had at the two previous dinners.

After this third dinner, the Chinese distributors chose to work less with this company. As time went on, they eventually located another foreign supplier of lobster, and chose not to work with the foreign company at all. By not understanding the application of Strategy Twenty-Six the foreign company lost their business in China.

EXAMPLE ONE
Guarding yourself against Strategy Twenty-Six

Strategy Twenty-Six is not to be perceived as a strategy against you, rather a strategy to assist you in getting a message through a third party. If you observe the applications of Strategy Twenty-Six, it is a great way to be warned before you make a mistake. The main thing is for you to know how to react when this strategy is applied on you. Chinese people are concerned about saving 'face', and because 'face' is so culturally important, they also want to save your 'face'. In this scenario it would have been a good idea for the foreign company to learn some Chinese cultural rules before conducting business in China. Even if you have a sought-after product you cannot rely on Chinese business people to be interested in your product when you continue to behave in a culturally inappropriate manner.

It is also a good idea to understand what your competitors are doing because you can be sure you are not the only company exporting your product to China. When Strategy Twenty-Six was applied on this company, instead of acting in a Western way, they could have taken the message as a prompt to learn and change their behaviour to be culturally appropriate.

When the message was sent to the foreign senior managers, the Chinese distributors were still keen to import this foreign company's lobsters into China. It was culturally appropriate to use a third party with lesser authority to help the two senior managers achieve a successful outcome with the Chinese distributors. The advice is to go with Strategy Twenty-Six without questioning its application or feeling judged.

EXAMPLE TWO
Strategy Twenty-Six in action (against you)

Chinese parents can be obsessively concerned about their children's safety and academic progress. Chinese parents will go to great lengths to have their children educated in a reputable place. Additionally, entry to a Chinese university is hugely competitive, and it is believed the more skills a child has acquired at a very young age the better their chances will be when they are older. Early childhood education is therefore very popular in China, and especially in kindergartens offering a contemporary Western curriculum.

In this scenario a foreign company specialising in

English-language early childhood education established a high-quality kindergarten in Chengdu, capital of Sichuan Province. To do so, the set up of a joint venture with a Chinese company with solid *guanxi* in Chengdu. *Guanxi* is explained in Book Two – *Deceive the Dragon: Negotiating to retain power*. The closest translation to *guanxi* is 'relationship' or 'connections'. The kindergarten, in an upmarket area of the central business district, has been operating successfully for three years. During its first year there were considerable set-up costs. In the second year the centre was fully operational, and by year three they had 200 children enrolled, with solid relationships and a good reputation among Chinese parents.

The foreign company had sent a general manager from their own country to oversee the operations in Chengdu. This person spoke little Mandarin Chinese. However, they were able to get by with the help of the bilingual Chinese office staff, employed by the Chinese joint venture partner. The general manager worked closely with Chinese office staff and felt no need to understand the language or the culture.

The company rented a three-storey building, with the kindergarten on the middle, or second floor, which had large rooms and copious natural light. The foreign company wanted high-quality fixtures, so they spent a lot of money on infrastructure. The ground floor was dark with no natural light and poorly shaped rooms, so it was used mainly for storage. In China, the first floor is at street level. The third floor was used for the company's administration.

To get to the second floor where the kindergarten was situated, the children had to climb a small flight of stairs.

Even though there had been no accidents, the parents considered these stairs unsafe. Also, the parents did not want their children to touch the handrails as they climbed the stairs because they considered this to be unhygienic.

Not wanting to complain to the general manager directly, the parents let the Chinese office staff know about their concerns. In this way the parents applied Strategy Twenty-Six *'to discipline, control, or warn'* the general manager. The Chinese office staff raised the parents' concerns over the location of the kindergarten with the general manager. Lacking deeper cultural knowledge, the general manager only partially understood what the Chinese staff were saying, and decided better cleaning was the answer. When it was clear that the general manager had not understood the full significance of the message, the Chinese office staff went to the Chinese joint venture partner for help.

They informed the joint venture partner about the parents' concerns. The joint venture partner then delicately discussed the issue with the general manager *'without directly naming names.'*

The general manager was shocked and quite annoyed that what seemed like a small matter had gone from a group of parents to the office staff and then to the joint venture partner. The Chinese partner told the general manager that the parents involved in this complaint had high-level connections. The Chinese partner suggested the best option was to move the kindergarten to the first floor while they improved the infrastructure. The Chinese partner was concerned that the general manager did not listen to the concerns with enough seriousness. The parents' strong connections with officials could result in the kindergarten being forced to move to the first floor with little warning.

As things would not happen in this way in the general manager's own country, they refused to move the kindergarten to the first floor, citing costs and the unsuitability of the rooms. They heard nothing for five months and then received notice from the government that they had to move the kindergarten to the first floor within a month. With little time to organise everything for the kindergarten to be fully operational in its new location the company ran into numerous difficulties. As a result of the disorder many parents were unhappy, and felt they were not getting value for money. The number of children attending the kindergarten dropped from 200 to 100. For the next year the kindergarten ran at a loss.

EXAMPLE TWO
Guarding yourself against Strategy Twenty-Six

In this situation it would have been beneficial for the foreign general manager to have developed an understanding of how Chinese business culture operates. Then they would have recognised Strategy Twenty-Six was in action and been able to respond in a more appropriate way. Greater understanding about the cultural aspects of the Chinese kindergarten market would also have been useful, as they would have a better knowledge of what was important to Chinese parents. When doing business with China it is crucial to recognise that what is important in your own culture may not be as important in the Chinese cultural framework, and vice versa.

Where Strategy Twenty-Six is applied, it is advisable to listen to these third-party messages. In Chinese culture, requests and expectations usually go via a third party and are rarely voiced directly. With greater understanding of Chinese culture, the general manager might have understood the stairs could be a problem, with Chinese parents not wanting to have their children touch stair rails for hygiene reasons.

Once Strategy Twenty-Six was applied, rejecting the feedback was detrimental to the business as there could have been time to respond by relocating the kindergarten much earlier. Listening to their Chinese business partner, as opposed to simply perceiving things from their own point of view, would have been a much better option. The overall advice is to listen to the message sent via Strategy Twenty-Six and act accordingly, instead of rejecting the information.

Key Points when Strategy Twenty-Six is used against you

- Recognise when you receive good advice, even though you may not appreciate hearing it.
- Receiving a cultural tip from your Chinese contacts on how to behave may be an indicator of their needs.
- Responding positively to critical feedback you receive from your Chinese contacts can prepare you for unexpected changes.

Example Three
Enacting Strategy Twenty-Six

In order to get something accomplished in China that requires you to confront a Chinese staff member, it is much more useful not to directly confront the Chinese person that you want to discuss things with. In this scenario you are managing an office in China and you are not happy with the way in which some of your Chinese staff members are communicating with your non-Chinese staff. To assist them in changing their behaviour it is much more useful to tell their colleagues, so that their colleagues will inform them of this issue. This must not be communicated in an accusatory way, rather, it needs to be conveyed in a caring manner.

In this scenario you have set up a joint venture with an architectural firm in China, and you are managing the office in Shanghai. You manage ten Chinese architects in the Shanghai office. Half of this Chinese team have studied in foreign countries and are aware of the differences between working in a Western office and a Chinese office. The other half of your Chinese team have only studied in China and have not travelled to other parts of the world. They are highly skilled architects. However, although they speak English, they do not know how to effectively communicate in an office managed by a Western person or how to effectively communicate with Western clients.

The company is involved in several design projects for companies building commercial properties in Shanghai and Beijing. Many Western clients come to the office for meetings. All the Chinese architects in the company need to communicate with Western business people for meetings. The Chinese architects who are not aware of Western business communication styles address the clients by using their family names. The Western manager would prefer the Chinese staff to greet Western clients by using their given names. Chinese culture is hierarchical, and it is considered impolite to greet someone who is perceived to be of a higher authority than you by their given name. Staff in China are much more guided by the senior members of the team regarding the projects. This is different to a typical Western business environment, where staff often work on projects with very little direct guidance. In fact, this level of independence is welcomed by staff in Western office environments. The need for constant guidance is an issue that the Western manager has found quite annoying.

To get the message across to the Chinese staff members who have little experience with Western business culture, they apply Strategy Twenty-Six. They talk with one of the Chinese architects who understands Western culture. They discuss how they would prefer all the staff to address Western clients in a more informal way, which includes calling clients by their given name. The Western manager applied Strategy Twenty-Six '*without directly naming names*.' By discussing the issue in this way, they know the staff members in question will be informed. Their objective is to '*discipline others*' in an indirect manner, so they will not cause 'loss of face'. After two weeks, the Chinese employees who were using Chinese family names to greet clients began to use the clients' given names. The Western manager observed that this was a difficult way of communicating for them and complimented them on the new way they addressed the clients. This is an excellent way of 'giving face' to the Chinese staff members.

The Western manager knew it would be difficult for the Chinese staff to work independently on projects with minimal guidance and organised a meeting to address this. The meeting involved every employee coming up with an idea for a new building design. They were simply given pencils and paper. The concept of this meeting had been relayed to the Chinese staff members who understood Western culture, so they pre-warned the staff members who needed to learn this. All staff members were given the opportunity to demonstrate their individual skills and were praised at their achievements by the management team. Strategy Twenty-Six had been successfully applied and reached its desired outcomes.

Negotiating in a Western Environment

EXAMPLE FOUR
Enacting Strategy Twenty-Six

In this scenario you are the team leader of a small team working in an outbound call centre. Your team is required to make a high proportion of outbound telephone calls which are logged into a database. The business has developed team and individual Key Performance Indicators (KPIs), which are based predominantly on the number of their outbound calls. Yearly performance reviews which determine salary increases are largely governed by these KPIs. Your personal KPIs are based on these team results. You can monitor your staff's inbound and outbound calls individually to assess their productivity.

Upon review, you notice one of your staff members has a significantly lower number of outbound calls. This strongly suggests that this team member is not nearly as productive as the rest of your team. However, you are not sure if this low number of calls is due to distractions or poor time management. To address the situation, you apply Strategy Twenty-Six. To apply this strategy, even though the rest of your team appears to be more productive, you discuss this issue with everyone. *'To discipline, control, or warn others'* you organise a team meeting to discuss the productivity and processes that are in place. You convey to them that you want to ensure all members of the team are meeting their KPIs and reiterate the importance of achieving this goal.

By applying Strategy Twenty-Six you have communicated your message *'without directly naming names'*. In this way, you have avoided confrontation with the staff member with the lowest outbound calls and made sure not to target them or expose their inconsistencies to the rest of the team. A few weeks later you assess the team's productivity levels and notice all your staff's productivity levels have increased, especially the staff member in question. You have successfully applied Strategy Twenty-Six.

Key Points when using Strategy Twenty-Six

- Being indirect with your messaging can be highly effective.
- You can use allies or high-performing staff to help change the behaviour of other staff.
- Praise is critical when your indirect messages are taken up.

Feign madness but keep your balance
means "let them underestimate you, play dumb, then surprise them"

Hide behind the mask of a fool, a drunk, or a madman to create confusion about your intentions and motivations. Lure your opponent into underestimating your ability until, overconfident, he drops his guard. Then you attack.

---

*I*n 1398 when he was near his death, Emperor Hong Wu, the founder of the Ming dynasty, decreed that the throne would pass to his grandson, Hui Du. The emperor had six sons who were not happy about this decision. On Emperor Hong Wu's death his grandson was just sixteen years of age and had little experience in leadership. The uncles were not happy about their nephew taking the throne. His grandfather's advisor recommended that he should immediately eliminate his six uncles because they were very corrupt and would cause him problems. Each of the uncles and their sons were summoned to court and accused of corruption and planning to overthrow the young emperor.

During their trials the uncles were found guilty and stripped of any rank they had achieved. However, one of the uncles refused to be summoned. This uncle was the Prince of Shang. He protested, saying he was not guilty. He wanted to remain a free man. His overall plan was to overthrow the emperor and he knew if he remained free, he could do this, because the emperor was so young and inexperienced.

To overthrow the young emperor, he applied Strategy Twenty-Seven – **Feign madness but keep your balance.** He did this by '*hiding behind the mask of a fool*', running through the streets shouting, stealing food, and sleeping on the streets pretending to be insane. His objective was '*to create confusion about his intentions and motivations*'. The young emperor heard about the Prince of Shang losing his mind and truly believed his uncle was mentally unwell. He concluded his uncle did not pose a threat to his position as emperor. The young emperor decided to let this uncle remain free. To apply Strategy Twenty-Seven his uncle '*lured him into underestimating his ability*', and because the emperor believed his uncle really was insane, he ordered his guards to release the Prince of Shang's sons.

When Strategy Twenty-Seven was applied, the emperor had fallen into the trap and '*dropped his guard*'. The Prince of Shang was not insane. Quite the opposite, in fact. He continued his corrupt behaviour towards the young emperor. The Prince of Shang and his sons then spent time building Shang's army, and once strong enough they defeated the young emperor Hui Du, taking the throne.

When Strategy Twenty-Seven is applied, the strategist plays down their ability to create confusion. Once they are perceived as less capable than they really are, they show their real intentions. By the time they are ready to show their objective, their opponent has dropped their guard because they are under the impression there is nothing to be concerned about.

Negotiating with Chinese People

EXAMPLE ONE
Strategy Twenty-Seven in action (against you)

In this scenario a provider of healthcare technology has been approached by a Chinese company interested in licensing their software. The software operates a program that can manage the smart appliances in a house, such as electricity, and use the information to help monitor the overall health status of the residents. The technology is used to keep the elderly in their homes without needing to be moved into aged-care facilities. China has a fast-growing ageing population where such technology is attractive.

Three Chinese managers travel from China to visit the technology company. The Western company has conducted significant research on the Chinese managers and discovered that one of them is extremely knowledgeable in this kind of technology. When they arrive at the office of the Western company, the three managers are shown the specifications and operational systems of the technology. The Western company is aware that there is another company with similar technology based nearby. However, they believe there is no reason for concern as they have developed *guanxi* with the Chinese company.

The Western company is also very pleased that there is a person inside this Chinese company who is highly aware of how their products work because they envisage this will make things easier when implementing the technology. When the

Chinese managers visit, there is no evidence of any high-level knowledge, because they say very little. The Western company presume that if they were so knowledgeable, they would display their knowledge. As a result of the Chinese managers' quiet behaviour the Western company took the view that the Chinese managers did not understand the intricacies of the technology.

The Chinese company applied Strategy Twenty-Seven *'hiding behind the mask of a fool'*. They have lured the Western company into *'underestimating their ability'*, so the engineers in the Western company *'dropped their guard'* and gave the Chinese company much more detail than was required. Often, when Strategy Twenty-Seven is applied, the cleverer you are, the less you demonstrate your knowledge.

The Western company felt they had to explain things very clearly, to have the Chinese company continue to be interested in their product. After the successful application of Strategy Twenty-Seven the Chinese company had detailed information. They had also set up a meeting with the other technology company. They were then able to go to the competitor, asking many detailed questions, and armed with a lot of information about pricing and installation of the technology. The Western company had no idea that Strategy Twenty-Seven was being applied, and *'dropped their guard'* by disclosing far too much information. The Chinese company used the knowledge they learnt from the Western company about the technology, pricing, and logistics to negotiate a much cheaper price with the other company.

EXAMPLE ONE
Guarding yourself against Strategy Twenty-Seven

The Western company had done their research and knew that the aged-care sector was a growing market in China. However, research is just one step - albeit an important one. China is a large market full of expert negotiators and opportunistic business people. Remember, Strategy Twelve – **Seize the opportunity to lead a sheep away** from Book Two - *Deceive the Dragon: Negotiating to retain power*, is always in action in the Chinese business world. Strategy Twelve is where Chinese business people take advantage of every opportunity. So even though your product may be sought after in China, keep in mind you are generally not going to be the only company that supplies what you have. Do not view Chinese business behaviour through what you know of your own business world. Do not expect Chinese business people to operate in the way that Western business people operate. When you know a Chinese business person is knowledgeable about a product, it is reasonable to expect Strategy Twenty-Seven to be applied. The Western company should not have told their prospective clients so much detail about the product. Once the Chinese business people had this information, they then knew what to ask the competitor.

When the Chinese group met with the Western technology company, a more effective way of communicating would have been for the technology company to ask questions, as opposed to giving information away. These questions could have been used to reveal the Chinese expert's knowledge.

When asking questions, it is important not to be too direct. If there is silence, do not try to fill the space up with talk, even if you feel uncomfortable. Often, when trying to fill the silence it is easy to fall into the trap of giving away too much information. Know your boundaries and work out before the meeting how much information you are happy to provide to your potential clients.

Example Two
Strategy Twenty-Seven in action (against you)

In a scenario where you are the founder and owner of an architectural business, over the last five years your company has developed some good contacts in China. Your company employs thirty staff and is recognised as providing artistic boutique designs, which have been viewed with interest by Chinese companies. During the last three years you have completed two substantial projects in Shanghai.

You decide to employ some newly graduated people to introduce new ideas into the business. Also, as you are intending to conduct more work with China, you thought it would be wise to employ a Chinese architect. You employed three recently graduated architects, one of whom is Chinese. All three come from your local university and know each other well, as they studied together. The Chinese architect is somewhat quieter than your other staff members and you put this down to a cultural difference. To date, their work has been satisfactory, although they do not say much in meetings.

You have been advised by your local government that a group of five Chinese delegates plan to visit your city in two weeks' time. They are looking for an architectural firm to design a five-star hotel in Shanghai. This would be a great project for your company to win. You have been informed that they will be visiting two other architectural firms in your city, which means you have some competition. You have also been informed that they do not speak English, which means you will need an interpreter. Even though you have a Chinese staff member who speaks English, this does not mean they have interpretation skills. This is something you need to organise. In preparation you have already completed the Pronounce Mandarin – The Easy Way online course at **www.pronouncemandarin.com** and learnt how to pronounce the Chinese delegates' names correctly. The skill that you are not that experienced in is presenting. However, you will certainly do your best because this job in Shanghai would be fabulous to win.

In preparation to receive this group, you organise a meeting with ten staff members who will be involved in the China project. Your Chinese staff member is in this group. You talk about your limited knowledge in presenting and ask the group if anyone has presenting skills, as you would prefer a staff member who has the skills to do the presentation. No one in the meeting puts their hand up to present, so you are resigned to the fact that this is up to you. At this stage in the meeting your Chinese staff member applied Strategy Twenty-Seven, because they were '*hiding behind the mask of a fool'*. They wanted you to *'underestimate their ability'* and feel like you were the only one who had the ability to present. What you did not know is that your Chinese staff member had very good presenting skills. Unfortunately, you were only informed about their ability after the presentation, by their colleagues who went to university with them. The reason the Chinese staff member did not indicate that they had good presentation skills was because they were afraid the presentation would not come across perfectly and they did not want to 'lose face' in front of the Chinese group. However, it would have been much easier for them to present, because as they were a skilled presenter and a native Mandarin Chinese speaker, they would not have needed to use an interpreter. However, if your Chinese staff member just sat in the audience, they would be able to show their knowledge by commenting and asking the right questions to the Chinese group. This format would guarantee them 'face' in front of the Chinese group.

So, *'after you had dropped your guard'* during your presentation, your Chinese staff member spoke up. They were quite vocal and made some intelligent comments. Unfortunately, due to the overly long and low quality of your overall presentation, your competitors won the project in Shanghai. When leaving your office, the Chinese group specifically complimented your Chinese staff member on their knowledge of the subject. Your Chinese staff member was happy because they gained 'face'. However, this was not the objective of the meeting and you were disappointed at losing such a good opportunity.

EXAMPLE TWO
Guarding yourself against Strategy Twenty-Seven

'Face' is a cultural component that is deeply engrained in Chinese culture. Generally, your Chinese staff will take any available opportunity to gain 'face' in front of other Chinese people. Unlike most Western business people, a Chinese person will often play down their level of skills. There are several ways in which the employer could have given the Chinese staff member 'face' instead of the Chinese group giving them 'face'. After researching the extent of the Chinese staff member's array of skills, it would have been good to acknowledge them in the team meeting, by saying their skills in presenting are invaluable to the company and the chances of securing this exciting and lucrative project. Following the presentation to the Chinese group, the employer could then hold a meeting with the rest of the team and praise the Chinese architect in front of the team, which would be a large 'face gainer'.

In order not to get trapped by Strategy Twenty-Seven it is important to understand why a Chinese staff member would not disclose what they really know. 'Face' is something a Chinese person is always searching for. If you can give your Chinese staff 'face' as opposed to an outside business doing so, it will be of benefit to the development of your business.

Employing a Chinese person can be a great asset to your company, especially when developing business connections in the Greater China Region. However, do not expect them to speak about their skills openly. In this scenario there was a 'face'-seeking element. If the employer knew the Chinese staff member was a good presenter, this staff member could have presented and there would have been no need to use an interpreter.

Key Points when Strategy Twenty-Seven is used against you

- Understand the full extent of the skills and capacity of your Chinese staff and/or contact.
- Spend quality time listening to your Chinese contacts and avoid talking too much.
- Plan how to give your Chinese staff 'face'.

EXAMPLE THREE
Enacting Strategy Twenty-Seven

When visiting a business that is owned and operated by Chinese people with whom you want to do business, either in your own country or in China, you are likely to have Strategy Four – **Wait Leisurely for an Exhausted Enemy** from Book One – *Tame the Tiger: Negotiating from a position of power.* played out on you. This is where the person who applies this strategy has a primary objective, which is to wear you down. If you know about this strategy, and therefore know when it is going to be applied on you, you can use Strategy Four as a pre-cursor to the application of Strategy Twenty-Seven. A scenario where Strategy Four is likely to be applied is when you visit a Chinese company, and they pick you up at the airport. During the conversation from the airport to your hotel, if they ask you when your flight home is leaving you can answer with an incorrect date, which is two days before you are really leaving. The night before the incorrect date of departure, there is a final discussion around the pricing of the product. The price that has been discussed throughout the negotiations is not viable, and so on what they believe to be the night before you are leaving, the Chinese contacts apply Strategy Four.

Thinking you are leaving the next day, they seek to exhaust you, hoping to negotiate the price they want. However, you do not care because you are not leaving the next day. You apply Strategy Twenty-Seven by '*hiding behind the mask of a fool*'. During the dinner you do not talk seriously about price. '*You have created confusion*', as they expected you to be nervous due to your imminent departure. However, they '*underestimate your ability*' regarding your knowledge about Chinese cultural issues, believing you will eventually give them the price they want. By the end of the night there is no resolution. You sense they are disappointed, because even though they have kept you awake until very late, taken you to three different entertainment venues, and made sure you are exhausted, you still have not agreed to their price. You thank them for the dinner and bid them farewell.

As your flight is really leaving in another two days, you call them the next day and tell them your flight has been delayed. You still do not tell them when you are leaving as they have already been fooled into thinking you are leaving on that day. Over the course of the negotiations you have had time to think about how you can secure a deal that suits you. You apply Strategy Twenty-Seven by focusing on ensuring you get the price you want and negotiating what you can compromise on, such as the delivery date and certain materials. You have had time to think about these issues, and how you can achieve the best deal. Through Strategy Four being applied on you, you have successfully applied Strategy Twenty-Seven.

Negotiating in a Western Environment

EXAMPLE FOUR
Enacting Strategy Twenty-Seven

In this scenario you graduated from university two years ago with a degree in economics, and have been working in a lower level role within a major bank for the last six months. You aspire to move up the ladder as quickly as possible, and there is a position opening up in the bank that will help you achieve your goals. However, you are aware that your current knowledge of economics is insufficient to fulfil the requirements of the role. You completed your undergraduate degree in economics and the position you wish to apply for requires some postgraduate knowledge in this subject, which you do not have. Ideally, you would like to read and learn the knowledge required. Unfortunately, there is not sufficient time to do this before the deadline for applications. The reality is that even if you did have time to read through the required information, you still may not have a deep enough understanding of the concepts to successfully demonstrate your knowledge.

When you attended university, you had an excellent university professor who was considered to be one of the most knowledgeable academics in the field of economics.

This university professor has always been very keen to help students achieve their future goals. You know that your university lecturer likes a particular Chinese restaurant, and you invite them to lunch so you can talk with the professor and get the information you need to fulfil the requirements of the position at the bank. To do this you apply Strategy Twenty-Seven and '*hide behind the mask of a fool*', so that you do not disclose any knowledge you already have. You want the professor to '*underestimate your ability*', so you can get as much information as possible and then confidently apply for the position. You do not display any great knowledge you have in economics to the professor, and instead ask many naive questions. You are aware that the professor likes to talk and teach about this topic, especially when someone has limited knowledge. Your carefully crafted style of communication results in the professor providing you with the necessary knowledge you require.

You now feel confident about applying for this position at the bank, and you present an excellent application. When you are interviewed for the position you are able to use the information you got from the professor to demonstrate that you have the breadth of knowledge that the application requires. By thinking this through and applying Strategy Twenty-Seven you successfully win this new position, and move up the career ladder.

Key Points when using Strategy Twenty-Seven
- Share only the essential information with your Chinese counterparts.
- Keep your real plans close to you, sharing only when necessary.
- There can be value in deciding to play the fool.

Lure your enemy onto the roof and then take away the ladder *means "to create situations that force the actions you desire"*

Using baits and deceptions, lure your enemy into treacherous terrain. Then cut off his lines of communication and avenues of escape. To save himself he must fight both your own forces and the elements of nature.

---

*D*uring the Warring States period, Han Xin was a general in the northern area of China. He was well known for his excellent application of Strategy Twenty-Eight – **Lure your enemy onto the roof and then take away the ladder**. Han Xin had defeated the Wei Kingdom, and was confident and ready to suppress another two rebellions to stay in power. His army was strong, and he was a clear-thinking strategist. As his army was approaching the river Wei, he found himself pursued by a third rebel faction, which he had not anticipated. This third rebellion was led by General Long Chu, whose army consisted of 300 soldiers. These soldiers were sent to intercept General Han Xin's path forward. In this situation General Han Xin was outnumbered. However, he refused to accept defeat, so he applied Strategy Twenty-Eight. His plan was to '*lure General Long Chu's army into treacherous terrain*'. To do this he ordered some of his men to go upstream and dam the river with sandbags. He was aware that to win in this situation he had to *'fight the forces of Long Chu's army and the elements of nature.'*

Overnight the river Wei dried up, making it easier for General Han Xin's army to cross. General Han Xin knew that Long Chu wanted to defeat his army and that they too would cross the river as soon as they could to implement this plan. As soon as Long Chu's army ventured onto the riverbed, General Han Xin ordered his army to remove the sandbags. He did this to *'cut off Long Chu's army's lines of communication'*. When Long Chu's army were just halfway across the river, the river was in its full force and many of his army drowned in the strong flowing river. Han Xin's army set out to eliminate the remainder of Long Chu's army as they were trying to flee. General Han Xin successfully applied Strategy Twenty-Eight because he prevailed in what seemed an impossible fight against the third rebellion. With this success he continued to maintain power over the Wei kingdom.

When applying Strategy Twenty-Eight, the strategist uses their resources to take their opponent out of their comfort zone and place them in a vulnerable situation where they have few skills or are unable to escape. Removed from their comfort zone, they need to use all their resources to escape, and will eventually exhaust themselves.

Negotiating with Chinese People

In this scenario you are selling high-quality wine to China. Your buyer works in Shandong, and most of your wine is sold in the city of Qingdao. Qingdao is famous for its beer and prides itself on making Chinese wine. While their beer has become famous across the world their wine is yet to gain international accolades. You have been exporting your wine into China for one year and, so far, everything has been running smoothly. You met your wine importer in Shanghai at a trade show where you had a booth to showcase your wine.

The Chinese buyers tasted your wine at the trade show and thought your wine was excellent. Your buyers visited your winery in your own country and were very impressed with the concept of the cellar door, which is essentially a designated space where wine can be sampled. There are generally two people who work at a cellar door to assist people taste the wine. At this stage, your knowledge of wine far exceeds your Chinese buyers' knowledge of wine.

On their visit to your winery they are curious about the intricacies of the tasting process and the making of wine. You enjoy sharing your knowledge. Your thinking is that the more knowledge they have about wine the more successful they can be in selling your wine. Unbeknown to you, they are applying Strategy Twenty-Eight. You are aware that they aspire to grow high-quality grapes in Shandong province.

You do not see this as a threat, though, because for this dream to come to fruition they would need years of practice to grow grapes and make a high-quality wine.

Your Chinese buyers approach you about opening a cellar door in Qingdao because they see this as a great way to advertise your wine. You believe this suggestion is an excellent idea. They inform you that they have good *guanxi* with someone who owns a property that would be a perfect location for a cellar door. This property is in a high-class area in Qingdao and you will not be charged rent. The deal is that they supply the cellar door with two Chinese staff who can speak some English, which will be a great asset because Qingdao is an international city, as it is likely that there will be foreigners visiting the cellar door.

Your job is to train the Chinese staff to work in a cellar door and to increase their knowledge of wine. When they apply Strategy Twenty-eight on you, they have '*lured you into opening up a cellar door in China*'. Things are going very well for the first year. The Chinese staff learn a lot about your wine over this time, which pleases you. There is constant communication between you and your importer via a video conferencing platform to see how the business is progressing. Then on one of your regular calls they inform you that there has been a change in circumstances, and their contact who has been able to give you free rent now has to charge you. You do not perceive a problem with this, as the business is earning quite well, and you think you will be able to afford the rent. They '*cut off your lines of communication and avenues of escape*' by telling you the rental is very high.

It will be impossible for you to pay the proposed rent. Your strategy is to ask your contact if they can locate a suitable place to relocate the cellar door. They agree to help you, and you think finding another suitable place for the cellar door is in their best interest. However, you do not realise they are applying Strategy Twenty-Eight.

After one month they do not locate any suitable properties that are affordable. In fact, the properties they found are even more expensive than the original cellar door location. This gives you no option but to close your cellar door in China and go back to exporting your wine without the cellar door. During the year of your contact's staff working in the cellar door they have gained a lot of information about your wine. A year later you are informed that they have opened their own cellar door using the knowledge they learnt from you. Their cellar door is the front for five high-quality foreign wines. This means you are now just one of several wine companies. Your Chinese buyers have successfully applied Strategy Twenty-Eight.

EXAMPLE ONE
Guarding yourself against Strategy Twenty-Eight

In the first instance do not think you are untouchable just because your product is of high quality. Although you may be selling a superior product, it is important to remember you are dealing with extremely sophisticated highly skilled negotiators.

When offered free rent, it would have been helpful to factor the real cost of rent into the budget, so if you are eventually charged it will be affordable. Even if something is given to you free of charge in China, it is likely that eventually you will have to pay. Taking more control, by employing your own Chinese staff to operate the cellar door, would have also given you more power. Sometimes, the idea of employing Chinese staff yourself, when you have a Chinese partner who offers to do this, seems all too difficult. Even though it may be difficult in the beginning, it is better in the long run as you will have more control. The differences between the Chinese business environment and the Western business environment is that Western people want to be experts in a field before they open a business. On the other hand, for Chinese business people it is the 'business skills' that are vital as opposed to having knowledge of the products they are selling, and in this instance the product was wine. Although they had little knowledge of wine, this did not stop them. Remember, you are dealing with a foreign culture who are constantly thinking strategically about how they can grow their business.

EXAMPLE TWO
Strategy Twenty-Eight in action (against you)

Your family business has been exporting barley to China for over a decade. Your barley is high quality, and the climatic conditions in your country have perfect growing conditions. Dealing with a family business has always appealed to your Chinese importers. They use your barley for their beer, and both your barley and their beer have a global reputation for being of excellent quality. In the past decade there have been some cultural differences. You believe you have addressed these successfully due to your knowledge of Chinese business culture. Additionally, because you know your product is the best in the world you are confident the Chinese importer will continue to purchase your barley. You believe your barley is the reason this Chinese beer tastes so good.

What you do not realise is that to gain a higher profit margin, your Chinese buyers have applied Strategy Twenty-Eight on you. You understand that your Chinese buyers have enjoyed low port charges, not realising you have been *'lured into exporting to China'* with these cheap port charges. Therefore, your Chinese buyers have been able to give you a good price for your barley. It had not occurred to you that these port charges may rise.

Your Chinese buyers discuss with you that the port charges have risen considerably, without revealing to you the actual figure. As a result of these inflated port charges, they tell you that they are being forced into a situation where they will have to pay less for your barley. The price they propose to purchase your barley is very low and gives you *'no avenue'* to make a profit. You decide to find other international markets to export your barley. China is such a large market that you need at least three other markets to equal the exports you were making to the Chinese market. You locate countries that have reasonably priced port charges and can pay you a price that will give you an acceptable profit margin. This means you need to handle the exports into three countries instead of one country.

After you take your barley elsewhere, the Chinese importer of your barley purchased other lower quality barley from other countries, meaning that their beer will also be of a lower quality. To incorporate this lower quality product the Chinese company slowly integrated this inferior barley into their beer. To do this they applied Strategy One – **Fool the emperor to cross the sea** from Book One – *Tame the Tiger: Negotiating from a position of power*. This strategy is used to hide the true intentions of the strategist. In this case the true intention is to create a cheaper product. They did this by simply acting as if the beer was no different. They now have a cheaper, inferior barley product as one of the key ingredients in their world-renowned beer. However, because they implemented the change to the inferior product slowly, consumers did not notice. The port charge increases were going to be implemented over time, it was simply the application of Strategy Twenty-Eight that gave the impression the changes were taking place all at once. This was a shock for you, and you could not see any way out of this situation. You had no way of finding out the truth because you had always left the communication regarding any changes in China to your Chinese buyers. They had '*cut off all lines of communication*', and successfully applied Strategy Twenty-Eight.

Example Two
Guarding yourself against Strategy Twenty-Eight

Whenever dealing with Chinese business people, it is dangerous to become complacent and think you know all that is going on. The option of just accepting the lower price would be detrimental to your profits. A more useful strategy would be to look at what the Chinese importers are losing and use this deficit as a bargaining position. In any business dealings with China it is crucial to build your own *guanxi,* because by developing your *guanxi* you then have your own connections and are more able to keep track of any changes regarding costs and other issues. If you had knowledge of the rise in port charges before being informed by the Chinese importers, you would have been more prepared for the consequences.

The bargaining power in this situation was the quality of the beer, because without the high-quality barley the beer would not taste the same. Discussing this with the Chinese importer would have been useful, as they may have rethought their decision. The international reputation of a product is very important, and consumers are likely to notice changes. Instead of just accepting a lower price, you could have focused on the diminishing quality of the beer as a negotiating tactic. The high-quality barley you supply is not grown in China, and without access to this product, the quality of the beer goes down. By focusing on the quality of the beer you may have been able to negotiate a price that was more acceptable.

Key Points when Strategy Twenty-Eight is used against you
- It is critical to know your point of difference so you can remain strong.
- Anticipate that fortunate circumstances may not last.
- Never become complacent when doing business in China.

Example Three
Enacting Strategy Twenty-Eight

Strategy Twenty-Eight is often applied on Chinese students when they choose to leave China and study in a Western country. Chinese students are generally contacted by educational agents, or they may have attended an educational exhibition in China to learn about courses in other countries. Their initial plan is generally to study in a foreign country and then return to China with their new skills. The most significant difference between the Western and Chinese education systems is the structure. The Chinese education system is embedded in a hierarchical structure, heavily influenced by the ideology of Confucianism, whereas the Western education system operates on a much more egalitarian structure. In China, you are unlikely to call your lecturer, teacher, or manager by their first name. Chinese students often do not realise this difference until they arrive in a Western country to study. So, in the first instance they are '*lured into treacherous terrain*'. Even though they may be constantly communicating with their family in China, as they are not physically in China '*their lines of communication are cut off*'. They are in a position where they have no choice but to live in an individualistic environment. Therefore, there is no '*avenue of escape*'.

When they first commence their education in a Western country they behave as they would in China, which can make it difficult for them to operate effectively. Generally, after one to two years, they become more comfortable with the Western mindset, especially as this individualistic way of life can give them more personal freedom. Their Chinese parents often become unhappy with the more individualistic behaviours their child has adopted. Typically, Chinese parents are the decision-makers regarding the courses their children study, and their future career plans. These plans usually include their children returning to China when they have completed their studies. However, it is often the case that when the Chinese students graduate, they are offered employment in the Western country where they have studied. Many businesses in Western countries employ Chinese students after they graduate, taking advantage of their cross-cultural and bilingual skills. The students often do not want to give up an individualistic lifestyle. Unbeknown to them, or their parents, Western educational institutions are continually applying Strategy Twenty-Eight by '*luring Chinese students into a Western lifestyle*'.

Negotiating in a Western Environment

EXAMPLE FOUR
Enacting Strategy Twenty-Eight

When building a house, many consumers are routinely caught out unexpectedly by the application of Strategy Twenty-Eight. This is applied by luring potential clients through display homes, where they view all the luxury items the builder has to offer. Once the consumer has chosen their favourite plan '*their lines of communication are cut off*' because they become emotionally attached to their potential dream home. Once emotionally attached, the builder discusses ideas and contracts. The consumer is left with the expectation that they will receive the same luxurious look as in the display home. However, upon review of their chosen house plan the consumer quickly discovers the basic package does not include the high-quality fittings they became very attached to. Often, at this point of the discussion, the consumer decides to upgrade and include the higher quality fittings, which is the goal of the building company. They have successfully lured the consumer into becoming emotionally attached, and therefore the customer sees no other option but to choose the more expensive plan.

Key Points when using Strategy Twenty-Eight

- Increase customers' purchases by engaging them emotionally in your products.
- Show people appealing ideas and they will be unlikely to go back to their old ways.
- Look at what is important to each customer so you can upsell.

Tie silk blossoms to the dead tree
means "to appear more powerful than you actually are"

Tying silk blossoms to a dead tree gives the illusion that the tree is healthy. Through the use of artifice and disguise, something of no value is made to appear valuable, something of no threat is made to appear dangerous, and something of no use is made to appear useful.

*L*ong ago in China, the hunter Li Hua had to leave his home to get food for his family. He would be gone for at least five days. His wife, Mei Hong, stayed at home to look after the house. Li Hua was rather anxious leaving Mei Hong by herself for five days, as she was five months pregnant with their first child. However, Li Hua knew that Mei Hong was a good decision-maker, and had often been left alone while he went hunting. If there was an unforeseen situation, Li Hua knew Mei Hong would be capable of dealing with it.

On the second day of Li Hua's absence, there was an unexpected knock at the door. Mei Hong opened the door to a man she did not know, who barged his way into the house and sat down on the chair in the lounge area. At that point she intuitively knew the man planned to rob their house. The man insisted that because it was approaching night-time, she should let him stay at the house. Out of the corner of her eye she caught a glimpse of her husband's shoes under the bed, giving her the idea to apply Strategy Twenty-Nine – **Tie silk blossoms to the dead tree, by** using '*artifice and disguise to make something of no threat appear dangerous*'. She conveyed to the man that she understood how important the kindness of strangers was to travellers. She told him she would give him a cup of tea, some water to wash his feet, and a pair of house shoes to wear for the evening.

Mei Hong went to the bedroom, got six pairs of her husband's house shoes, and placed them on the floor next to the man's feet. The man was confused, informing Mei Hong that he only needed one pair of shoes. However, the many pairs of shoes merely '*gave an illusion*' of abundance. Mei Hong explained to the man that only one of the pairs of shoes was for him, and the others were for her husband and four relatives who would soon be arriving at the house. They would need shoes as soon as they arrived, as night was approaching, and their feet would be cold without shoes. Mei Hong created the situation with '*no threat to appear dangerous*', explaining to the man she was pleased to prepare the evening meal for him, her husband and the four relatives. She communicated her delight that they could all eat together. She invited him to sit and rest while she went into the kitchen to cook. The man realised his plans, which were to wait until Mei Hong was sleeping and then to steal valuable items from the house, would not work. When Mei Hong went into the kitchen, he quietly ran away. Mei Hong had successfully applied Strategy Twenty-Nine. When Li Hua returned from his hunting expedition, he congratulated his wife on being such a clever strategist.

Strategy Twenty-Nine is applied using props, facades, and camouflage. The objective is to ensure your opponent remains unclear of your strengths and weaknesses.

Negotiating with Chinese People

EXAMPLE ONE
Strategy Twenty-Nine in action (against you)

You have a medical product with a digital application and want to market this product to China. Your company has been manufacturing medical equipment for twenty years, so you are very experienced in your field. Some contacts in your country have introduced you to a Chinese business person whose company may want to market your product across China. Although your contact has not specifically used this Chinese company, they have heard from other sources that the company is well known and may be interested in your product. You meet the Chinese contact through a video conference call and are impressed with the information they provide you with.

They take you on a journey by showing you their website. The photos on their website include large hospitals in China, and they inform you of their solid connections in these hospitals. The person representing the company speaks English, which pleases you, although the website is in Chinese. The language issue does not concern you as you can view many photographs on the website and are extremely impressed with what they show you. By showing you these large-scale hospitals in China they are applying Strategy Twenty-Nine by '*tying silk blossoms to a dead tree*', which gives the illusion that their business is very large. '*Through the use of artifice and disguise*' they make their business '*appear valuable*'.

The application of Strategy Twenty-Nine has seduced you into believing that their business is really working with these large hospitals, which is not true. They inform you that they have excellent connections with the hospitals, although they do not tell you they are actually working with the hospitals in the images on their website - you just assume this.

They make it seem so easy to sell your medical products into China. The company requires a monthly fee, which seems reasonable. They also offer you a substantial discount if you pay one year in advance. You take up this offer and make the annual payment. After making this payment you hear very little from them. After six months has passed you realise you are only receiving very occasional communications and have not made any sales. You realise their business is not as you thought it was. They have successfully applied Strategy Twenty-Nine, by making their business look much bigger than it is.

EXAMPLE ONE
Guarding yourself against Strategy Twenty-Nine

Believing whatever you see and not questioning the veracity of things is a sure way of coming out second best in China. Just because a product is sought after in China does not automatically mean that a Chinese company will want to import and distribute your product. Popular products will result in many other businesses from across the globe trying to sell similar products into China. It is always a good idea to know what the popular products are, and to ensure you never become complacent by thinking you are the only company with this product.

In this situation, a business colleague merely said they had heard this Chinese company was good. However, they had not actually worked with them. In China, to manage your risk, you are advised to talk with at least three distributors before deciding which one to go with, as this will provide useful comparisons. This company showed their website and said they had connections in these large hospitals. There was no talk of the Chinese company working with these hospitals. Contacting these hospitals and seeing if the Chinese company were distributing to them would have been useful research.

Paying money so easily was not a good move. This displays to the Chinese company that you do not have the ability or the desire to negotiate.

Example Two
Strategy Twenty-Nine in action (against you)

In this scenario you are a sought-after wine producer. Your wine makers have perfected a range of fine wines, and your product is now a famous brand in your own country. As a result, you are ready to export to China. A Chinese delegation visited your city and your local government department asked you to be a part of this visiting delegation. You saw as a great opportunity to introduce your wine. They wanted the Chinese delegation to visit your winery and for you to host the delegation for a short time on your property, which you were thrilled about because this was a great opportunity for personal introductions.

The Chinese delegation consisted of three people, two men and one woman, whose wine knowledge was extensive. These three people from China visited your winery and stayed for a couple of hours to talk with you and your staff. They requested a return visit the following day before they returned to China. You saw this as a good sign, as you believed it indicated they had an interest in your product.

On the second visit they were curious about the history of your winery and wanted to see the awards you had won. They also asked you questions about yourself, which revealed your likes and dislikes. These questions included your choice of colours. This was easy to answer, as your preferred colour is red, relating to red wine. There was also a lot of discussion about food and you discussed how you liked seafood. The discussion about travel came up, and because you live in a rural environment you told the group how you like to stay in a quiet part of a hotel when you travel, as you are so accustomed to only the noises of nature on your property. Throughout this discussion they were applying Strategy Twenty-Nine using '*artifice and disguise*' because they were keen to import your wine into China and planned to buy it for a good price. They wanted their company to '*appear valuable*' so you would seriously consider dealing with them. For the following two months after they returned to China, you continued to communicate with them. You then visited the group in Shanghai, where they were based. You organised meetings with three other distributors, although you put more time and effort into the group that had visited you in your own country, because you had begun developing a solid relationship.

The Chinese company that visited you in your own country offered to organise your hotel. You were pleased about this, because being a first timer to China, you had no idea of locations in Shanghai. They picked you up at the airport in a red BMW, which is your favourite colour. You were under the impression that this was their car and were pleased by their similarity in your tastes. They drove you to the hotel, where it appeared, they had good *guanxi* at the hotel. They organised a very quiet room for you, making a joke that you need this because you live in a rural location. They also took you to a seafood restaurant. You were delighted because the trip appealed to all your desires. Following this first day in China you felt good about this company and decided to contract them to import your wine. You do not realise that they have applied Strategy Twenty-Nine *'through the use of artifice and disguise'*, in order to become the importer of your wine. Most of what you experienced was an illusion. They had hired the red BMW for the day, and because you had told them about your likes and dislikes regarding hotels and food it was easy for them to provide experiences that appealed to you.

Although you had three other meetings in Shanghai, you just went through the motions at these meetings and had no intention of appointing any of the other companies as your wine distributor. After six months of working with your chosen company one of your business colleagues informed you that the companies you decided against would have probably given you a much better price for your wine. On your next visit Shanghai to meet with the distributor you did not see a red BMW, or have a quiet room organised, or get taken out to a seafood restaurant.

By appealing to you on an emotional level in the initial meetings, you were convinced that this first wine distributor was the best one, and therefore did not give the other distributors the opportunity to discuss price and other distribution issues. Strategy Twenty-Nine was successfully applied by the first wine distributor, because you made your decision on an emotional level.

Example Two
Guarding yourself against Strategy Twenty-Nine

Remember, when dealing with China you are always in a competitive market. China is a large market and many countries export to China. When the Chinese delegation visited the winery and asked you many questions, the answers revealed your likes and dislikes. There is nothing wrong with answering these questions honestly. However, it is important to know that the reason you are being asked these questions is for the Chinese company to apply Strategy Twenty-Nine. Be mindful of what you tell Chinese business people because the information you disclose is often used as research to prepare for the application of Strategy Twenty-Nine. In Chinese business culture everything has a purpose, and innocent questions which appear to be small talk are often research about you. When a Chinese company is relatively small, and they are keen to deal with you because you have a product they want, they will often make their business look larger than it actually is, which is the application of Strategy Twenty-Nine.

Strategy Twenty-Nine is different to Strategy One, which is about making a situation familiar or comfortable, while Strategy Twenty-Nine is about making something appear other than it really is. It is always a good idea to meet with other distributors, and to treat them as if they are just as important as the company that has previously impressed you, otherwise you will be consumed by Strategy Twenty-Nine. Remember, the glamour of Strategy Twenty-Nine is short-lived, and to guard yourself against it you need to see through the illusion.

Key Points when Strategy Twenty-Nine is used against you

- Ensure you always make decisions about the growth of the business, rather than being swayed by what you personally like and dislike.
- Compare all the available distributors' offerings before you select a distributor.
- Look beyond the appealing decorations to see the real situation.

EXAMPLE THREE
Enacting Strategy Twenty-Nine

In general, any company that you deal with in China will be larger than most businesses from Western countries. Quite often, a company that would be defined as a small business in China would be regarded as a large business in a Western country. Western businesses are more likely to be exporting boutique products to China, rather than mass produced products. Western companies will often specialise in a particular product, and will be experts in their field, with years of experience. When trying to attract a larger Chinese company to sell your product to Chinese people Strategy Twenty-Nine is an excellent strategy to use. '*Tying silk blossoms*' onto your business will provide '*the illusion*' that your business is larger than it really is.

In this scenario you are a real estate agent who wants to sell properties to Chinese customers. You have twenty staff. In the Chinese business environment, your company would be considered a small business. You want to market your services to large Chinese companies who have access to many Chinese business people and families wanting to invest in foreign countries. To apply Strategy Twenty-Nine, you create a network with seven other real estate companies from across your country, making the total number of eight companies working together.

This appeals to the emotions of Chinese people, because the number eight is considered a lucky number in Chinese culture. With '*artifice and disguise*' you have made your business look much larger, and also now have connections with real estate businesses across your country. This is likely to give your potential Chinese customers security, as their aim is to build solid *guanxi* so they can make recommendations to their friends and family about companies that can help them to buy property. This security comes from the apparent size of your company as well as your cultural knowledge. Once Chinese people establish solid *guanxi* they are likely to want to keep dealing with your company. For your potential Chinese customers, you can be introduced as part of this group of eight, and for your domestic business you can still appear as your own independent company with your twenty staff. Operating in this way will give your potential Chinese customers the image you need, to appeal to their cultural and business requirements.

Negotiating in a Western Environment

EXAMPLE FOUR
Enacting Strategy Twenty-Nine

Strategy Twenty-Nine can be successfully used in a Western business environment when a house has been advertised to sell. Real estate agents can use this strategy '*through the use of artifice and disguise*', to make the house for sale as aesthetically pleasing as possible. When preparing to advertise the house the real estate agent can take multiple photographs of the property from several angles, making sure they capture the best of the house. These photographs can be strategically filtered by using the skills of an expert photographer, who can create the illusion that the house is impeccable and without fault. However, the house may be well lived-in, with wear and tear throughout.

In the real estate business, Strategy Twenty-Nine can be used by putting in staged furniture and '*making something of little value appear valuable*'. A clever real estate agent will carefully select furniture that provides a contemporary spacious environment that will attract the consumer. As smell is our most archaic sense when something appeals to a buyer through attractive smells such as scented candles and baked goods this will create a welcoming space and a sense of comfort or homeliness. In this way the potential buyer is drawn in by the smell, which is intended to provoke a positive emotional response, thereby ensuring a better chance of concealing minor flaws in the property such as layout challenges, an aged bathroom, cracked walls, or old flooring. By applying Strategy Twenty-Nine, the real estate agent is *'tying silk blossoms on a dead tree'*.

Key Points when using Strategy Twenty-Nine

- Create positive emotional experiences to distract your customer from the negatives of your product.
- Use emotionally laden symbols and imagery, which speak more loudly than words.
- Engage you customer through their emotions to encourage them to purchase your product.

Exchange the role of guest for that of host *means "to act first as the guest and then gradually become more dominant"*

Defeat the enemy from within by infiltrating the enemy's camp under the guise of cooperation, surrender, or peace treaties. In this way you can discover his weaknesses and then, when the enemy's guard is relaxed, strike directly at the source of his strength.

*X*iang Liang was obsessed with power and wanted to be in a dominant position. He lived in the state of Chu where he was never able to rise to the top of the power structure. The state of Chu fell to the control of the Qin Dynasty. Xiang Liang was not happy being under the control of the Qin Dynasty. His nephew, Xiang Yu, was also unhappy with this new arrangement. Xiang Liang decided to flee to the state of Wu and seek asylum, and he took his nephew Xiang Yu with him. Xiang Yu had a great deal of respect for his uncle Xiang Liang.

After five years of living in Wu, Xiang Liang began to apply Strategy Thirty - **Exchange the role of guest for that of host**. He developed a solid reputation as a strong and clever leader by demonstrating his skills in organising people and building infrastructure. People regarded him as a great leader, and through his leadership he gained the trust of the people of Wu. He applied Strategy Thirty by *'infiltrating from within'* the community of Wu *'under the guise of cooperation'*. While building up this trust he taught his nephew Xiang Yu the cleverness of the 36 Strategies, because he required his nephew to help him successfully complete the application of Strategy Thirty.

The governor of Wu decided to attack the Qin Dynasty, because reliable sources had informed him the Qin Dynasty wanted to take over Wu. Noticing the high level of trust that Xiang Liang and his nephew had developed with the people of Wu, the governor asked them to lead his army in this attack. Xiang Liang and Xiang Yu accepted this challenge and met with the governor to discuss their plans. In the meeting the governor's *'guard was relaxed'*, which allowed Xiang Liang to *'strike directly at the source of his strength'*. In the middle of the meeting Xiang Liang instructed Xiang Yu to behead the governor of Wu. Xiang Liang then declared himself the governor of Wu, and because he had gained the trust of the people of Wu there were only a small number of people who objected. These people were killed, and Xiang Liang achieved his dream of becoming a leader through the application of Strategy Thirty.

Negotiating with Chinese People

EXAMPLE ONE
Strategy Thirty in action (against you)

In this scenario you have Chinese guests arriving to inspect your olive oil products. Your family business has been operating for thirty years. You are planning to export your olive oil to China. You are aware that the idea of a family business is likely to be appealing to Chinese business people.

The Chinese group consist of five people from Kunming, in Yunan Province. You have been informed that no one in the group speaks English, which means you must use an interpreter. Although you have had no experience working with interpreters you believe it will be easy because, in your understanding, the interpreter just needs to speak both Mandarin Chinese and English. Your city has a university that teaches many Chinese students, so you contact the university and are provided with one of their bilingual Chinese students for this job. This student comes from a business background, with parents who are distributors of food products in China. You feel this could be a good arrangement, as they understand the food sector.

You are not aware there are boundaries when working with an interpreter, and it is not as simple as using someone who is bilingual. The Chinese guests arrive, and your interpreter is very friendly and greets them. The interpreter begins applying Strategy Thirty '*by infiltrating*' your meeting. After the presentation of your product, the interpreter networks with your Chinese guests and they exchange contact details. You seem to have faded into the distance, and the interpreter becomes the important person. However, at this point you are grateful for the help of the interpreter. After the meeting, the interpreter explains to you that they have a lot of experience in this area because many members of their family are business people in China. The interpreter has '*discovered your weaknesses*', which are your limited knowledge of Chinese language and Chinese business culture. During this whole time *'your guard was relaxed'* because you know the interpreter knows a lot more about Chinese business than you do.

After the meeting you feel you need the interpreter's help to continue this relationship, so you offer them a small fee to assist you. The idea is that they will help you communicate with the Chinese distributors for the next couple of weeks, then hand the continuation of the relationship over to you. During these two weeks they do a lot of work for you. You are now in the position where you cannot successfully communicate with the Chinese distributors without the help of the interpreter. During this time, you have had very little contact with the Chinese distributors. You realise you have lost control of the situation and the only way you are going to keep this relationship moving forward with the Chinese distributors is to continue employing the interpreter. They now have a lot of information about your company, and knowledge about the olive oil industry.

After one year of dealing with the Chinese group you still have little control over what is going on. You are not concerned, though, as things are going smoothly. The Chinese distributors that you are dealing with inform you that the cost of marketing your products has risen, and they must negotiate a lower price to buy your products. As you have always left this up to your Chinese staff member you have no knowledge of how to negotiate with the Chinese distributors. Your Chinese staff member is closely connected with the Chinese group and they therefore do not want to 'lose face' by not accepting the lower price that the group is now offering for your product. You have little choice but to accept the lower price, because you do not know how to negotiate your way through this deal. By applying Strategy Thirty, the Chinese staff member, who was initially the student interpreter, has moved themselves into your company. When an issue arose, you had insufficient knowledge to deal with this situation.

By helping to make their opponents life easier the strategist can apply Strategy Thirty. Once the strategist feels they have gained some control over the situation, they then move forward with the objective of gaining more control. Once Strategy Thirty is fully implemented the strategist will have sufficient control so that their opponent cannot do without them.

EXAMPLE ONE
Guarding yourself against Strategy Thirty

There are clear rules and boundaries to put in place when using an interpreter that will protect you against the successful application of Strategy Thirty. Every industry has its own vocabulary and terminology. The interpreter should be briefed in the vocabulary of your industry so they can research the correct language. Briefing them on terminology gives you the upper hand, because you are demonstrating your knowledge in this area, in comparison with their limited technical knowledge. Strategy Thirty focuses on your weaknesses. In this situation your weaknesses are a limited understanding of the Chinese language and Chinese business culture. To counter these weaknesses, you need to draw attention to your strengths.

The interpreter should not network or exchange their contact details with your Chinese guests. After meeting with your guests, it is important to have a debriefing session with the interpreter. You may want to use their skills to communicate further with your potential Chinese clients. It is vital that you remain in control so that when issues arise, such as pricing, you can deal with them yourself because you have developed a strong relationship with the Chinese distributors.

Example Two
Strategy Thirty in action (against you)

In this scenario you and another person own a large retirement village. You both have a lot of experience in the retirement industry, and the village has made considerable profit over the last ten years. This retirement village has 100 units, and is located close to shops, transport, and medical facilities. In the last year there has been a dispute over how many hours your business partner works and how they are remunerated for this. They feel they have been working more hours in the business than you, and therefore deserve more profit. You have also been doing many things behind the scenes, without accounting for these extra hours. This tension is causing conflict, which you believe with the right professional help can be easily sorted out.

A Chinese group, consisting of a consortium of four people, visit your retirement village. They see this as a growing market in China and would like to explore what you are doing in your country. You become friendly with the Chinese group, and with one member of the group who speaks excellent English. You confide in this person that communication between you and your business partner has been somewhat strained. After hearing this news, they applied Strategy Nine – **Watching the fire from the opposite shore** from Book Two – *Deceive the Dragon: Negotiating to Retain Power.*

To apply Strategy Nine, they politely watch the situation unfold, then move towards applying Strategy Thirty. They continue to communicate with you for the next six months, then as a solution to your issue with your business partner they offer to buy your partner out of the business. This suits you and your business partner because the relationship has significantly deteriorated.

After buying your business partner out of the business they apply Strategy Thirty. The new business partnership gives them the opportunity to '*infiltrate your business*'. They '*discover your weakness*', which is your lack of organisational skills. Your business partner was always excellent at organising things, and while you were in partnership you never had to worry about that side of the business. As you have limited organisational skills '*your guard is relaxed*' with this aspect of the business, giving your Chinese business partners an opportunity to successfully apply Strategy Thirty.

Things go along well for one year with your new Chinese business partners. They then commence bringing in their own Chinese staff, informing you that this will be good for the business. They explain that the retirement village can now attract Chinese residents, as the Chinese staff will be able to converse with them. This is not what you had in mind. However, you want to be flexible, and agree this could be good for the business. After the new Chinese staff are given positions in the business, you discover the Chinese and Western staff have different ways of doing things. Further, the Chinese members of staff have limited English.

You do not realise that Chinese staff require more explicit directions to complete tasks, whereas Western staff are quite independent in organising their work. Only when the Chinese staff begin working in the business do you really experience your organisational deficits, because things become disorganised and you do not have the skills to fix these problems. Your Chinese business partners begin implementing new things, such as different furniture designs and social events for the long-term residents that are unfamiliar to them. After a two-year period, you have lost control of how the retirement village is operating. This is not the outcome you wanted. Your business partners gain more and more control over how the business runs. The original contract did not state that your new Chinese business partners could *not* implement these changes, and so there is nothing you can do or say. The whole atmosphere of the village has deteriorated due to the changes your Chinese business partners have implemented. They have taken control and placed you in a position where it will be difficult to regain control.

Example Two
Guarding yourself against Strategy Thirty

When the situation is stable, and the time is right, Chinese people usually make excellent business partners because they have extremely good negotiation and all-round business skills. It is important to understand your strengths and weaknesses. Disclosing your vulnerabilities lays the ground for the application of Strategy Thirty.

The deficit here was organisational skills, which allowed the Chinese business partners to implement several new structures in the retirement village. Understanding things are done differently in the Chinese business environment would have been useful information for the future of the partnership and the growth strategy of the retirement village. Just as many Western business people do not understand Chinese business practices, it cannot be assumed that Chinese business partners understand Western business practices either. There are key differences between how Chinese and Western staff behave in the workplace. In this scenario the Chinese business partners have been free to make decisions.

Training in how the retirement industry works in a Western country would have given the potential Chinese business partners clearer boundaries. Issues such as changes to the design and infrastructure of the retirement village should have been discussed before the contract was signed. This disorganisation provided an inroad for the application of Strategy Thirty, resulting in a loss of control.

Key Points when Strategy Thirty is used against you

- Understand your vulnerabilities so you cannot be taken advantage of.
- Know what is critical to retain command over.
- Learn how to work with an interpreter.

EXAMPLE THREE
Enacting Strategy Thirty

The best time to apply Strategy Thirty on your Chinese contacts is '*when they are relaxed*' and then you can '*infiltrate the situation*'. In this scenario you are a beef producer, and in your Western country your beef has the reputation of being extremely high quality. You own and operate three large farms. This is a family business, and there are several things that would be appealing to Chinese people, including your reputation as a high-quality beef producer, and the family business structure. In your own country a Chinese business contact introduces you to a group of Chinese business people. They consist of four people who deal in the meat import industry into China. You want to export your meat into China and are pleased when your business contact arranges to introduce you to these four people at a Chinese banquet. Your business contact positions you at the same table as the Chinese business people so you can get to know them. However, your business contact makes sure they have control over the conversations by being the intermediary in all conversation that takes place at the banquet. The group only speak very basic English. You have an advantage, in that you have completed the online course **www.pronouncemandarin.com** so you know how to pronounce their names correctly and say a few key words and phrases. This impresses them and gives you the confidence to apply Strategy Thirty. You exchange contact details with each of them through an online platform using the QR code on your phone.

After the dinner you then contact these four Chinese business people independently of your business contact. You individually host a meal for each one of them, and their families at a restaurant where your beef is on the menu. This gives you the opportunity to develop *guanxi*. You do not discuss business with them, rather you get to know them, and they get to taste your excellent product. You have applied Strategy Thirty, by bypassing your original contact. However, you ensure you always speak highly of this business contact, thus giving them 'face'.

After you have taken each of the distributors out for dinner you contact them, checking to see if they enjoyed the meal. You then set up another meeting with each distributor to discuss how you can work together regarding the distribution of your beef product into China. In this way, you can choose the right distributor, or preferably distributors, as it is always a good idea to have at least two distributors. In this situation, by applying Strategy Thirty, you do not have to go through a third party.

Negotiating in a Western Environment

EXAMPLE FOUR
Enacting Strategy Thirty

In this scenario Strategy Thirty can be used where your company, an accounting firm, recruits you as a new graduate accountant. A more senior accountant spends a substantial amount of time mentoring and coaching you and you quickly pick up the duties of the role. You are very ambitious and keen to move up in the firm. However, you are aware that your mentor is next in line for the managerial role. To use Strategy Thirty, you '*infiltrate*', by being patient and absorbing all the knowledge your mentor shares with you.

Building trust with this senior accountant is a crucial step towards the successful application of Strategy Thirty. '*When their guard is down*' you gain as much knowledge about the management team and their expectations as possible. You are aware that to move up the ladder in the accounting firm you need to impress the senior management team by building your portfolio of clients, which is one of the things your mentor has taught you to do.

Before long, your portfolio grows considerably larger than other members in your team, and you are regarded as a rising star within the firm. You have successfully applied Strategy Thirty by displaying your knowledge, resulting in you being promoted above your former mentor.

Key Points when using Strategy Thirty
- Know the right time to impress your Chinese contacts.
- Develop your own *guanxi* with Chinese business contacts.
- Spend time building up trust so you can have more control.

Your Next Steps

Having just finished reading *Endure the Tiger*, here are some suggestions for your next steps:

- Now I can plan my approach when I am negotiating in any situation.
- The 36 Strategies will help me when communicating with Chinese people.
- I will share this knowledge with my colleagues.
- I want to read *The Dao of Negotiation* series. I'll find them at **www.leoniemckeon.com**
- I will contact Leonie to:
  - Help me think completely differently about my business development challenges.
  - Deliver a presentation for my next conference or other event.
  - Deliver 36 Strategies workshops to my team.
- Because **Pronounce Mandarin - The Easy Way** is perfect for beginners, I will learn how to correctly pronounce Chinese names and some useful Mandarin Chinese words and phrases via **www.pronouncemandarin.com**

Go to **www.leoniemckeon.com** for more information about the 36 Strategies. Leonie has several informative videos and blogs to help you further your understanding of how to negotiate in any business environment.

WHAT PEOPLE SAY ABOUT WORKING
WITH LEONIE MCKEON

BEC HARDY WINES

"I can't tell you how much you have given our family, and me personally, through your insights about the 36 Chinese Strategies. Understanding how the 36 Chinese Strategies are applied in Chinese business culture was the lightbulb moment which has led to such revenue growth, opportunities and personal growth. This has been one of the great, exciting professional and personal journeys and achievements of my life. Thanks again."

Richard Dolan, Joint Managing Director

HATCH, Western Australia

"Anyone who has the pleasure of having dealings with China and the Chinese will find Leonie's 36 Chinese Strategies workshops invaluable. The workshops were eye-opening and had the right amount of humour and personal stories to more than keep our attention."

Denis Pesci, PDG Hub Director, Western Australia

Fletcher Building

"From a personal perspective, Leonie was instrumental to our Chinese cultural program developed for the Super Retail Group. The target audience for the workshop was our Management and Leaders from Logistics, Marketing and Category. In organising the program for the team, I found Leonie incredibly resourceful, totally understood the brief and built value-add to the program. Often you don't know what you don't know so great to have a Subject Matter Expert to guide and shape a very successful program."

Shirley Brown, Capability Development Manager –
Australian Distribution

Australian American Fulbright Commission

"The Art of Negotiation – 36 Strategies derived from 'The Art of War' workshop delivered by Leonie at the Australian Institute of Company Directors (AICD) challenged conventional thinking."

Peter de Cure, Chairman, Australian American Fulbright
Commission

Kmart

"The training that Leonie provided to our team was excellent. The program was practical, delivered with context, and opened the team members' minds to learning more about how to do better business in China. I have no doubt that what we have learned will be applied and will provide great outcomes for our business. Leonie has also provided a great personal development opportunity for members of our team."

Matthew Webber, International Supply Chain Manager

The Dao of Negotiation
The Path between Eastern Strategies and Western Minds

		Strategy Number
Book One – *Tame the Tiger*	Advantageous Strategies	1, 2, 3, 4, 5, 6
Book Two – *Deceive the Dragon*	Opportunistic Strategies	7, 8, 9, 10, 11, 12,
Book Three – *Lure the Tiger*	Strategies for Attack	13, 14, 15, 16, 17, 18
Book Four – *Bewilder the Dragon*	Confusion Strategies	19, 20, 21, 22, 23, 24
Book Five – *Endure the Tiger*	Strategies for Gaining Ground	25, 26, 27, 28, 29, 30
Book Six – *Flee the Dragon*	Strategies for Desperate Situations	31, 32, 33, 34, 35, 36

The Dao of Negotiation:
The Path between Eastern Strategies and Western Minds

by Leonie McKeon

More Control, More Success, More Wins!

Based on *The Art of War*, *The Dao of Negotiation* series unmask the 36 Strategies used in Chinese culture and business.

This incredible series of 6 books provide invaluable tips for any business person looking to improve their overall negotiation skills, as well as become better at negotiating with Chinese People.

Discover how you can use this ancient wisdom for more business success.

www.leoniemckeon.com

www.ingramcontent.com/pod-product-compliance
Lightning Source LLC
Chambersburg PA
CBHW071110210326
41519CB00020B/6247